D0503830

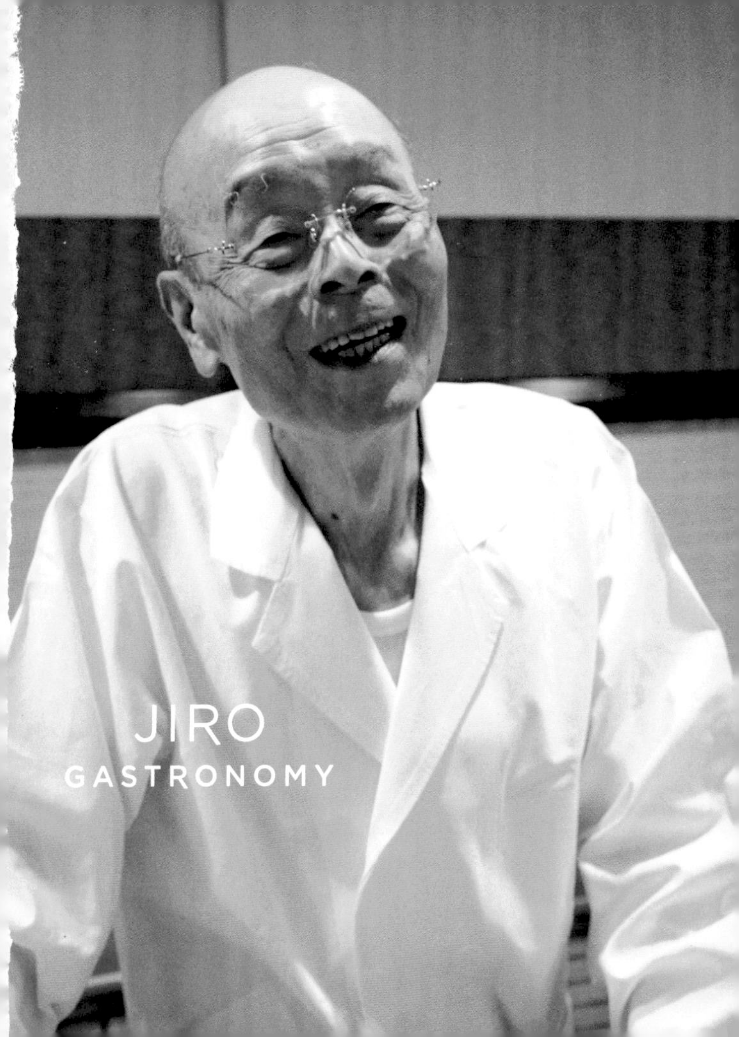
JIRO
GASTRONOMY

FOREWORD

This book introduces readers to the sushi varieties served throughout the year at Sukiyabashi Jiro and offers some recommendations on how to fully enjoy Edo-style sushi. Sushi originated as a casual food served at food stalls in the Edo era. Sushi chefs would brush *nikiri* soy sauce and *nitsume* (or *tsume*) sauce on top of the sushi pieces they made and then place the pieces in front of their customers. The customers would quickly eat the sushi with their hands, then drink some tea, wipe their hands on the noren curtains hanging at the entrance of the food stall, and leave.

Because of sushi's roots, conversing during the meal and sharing sake together, though fundamental to the origins of restaurants and pubs, is not customary in sushi houses. Sukiyabashi Jiro maintains the tradition of Edo-style sushi. We serve sushi that we want customers to enjoy as soon as it is prepared. Our reputation has spread, and now customers from around the world visit us every day. We are truly grateful. This book is dedicated to them and to everyone who has an interest in Sukiyabashi Jiro's sushi.

Jiro Ono

SUKIYABASHI JIRO

CHAPTER 1 Omakase Tasting Menu

Sole	かれい	9
Flounder	ひらめ	11
Juvenile Cuttlefish	しんいか	13
Golden Cuttlefish	すみいか	15
Juvenile Yellowtail	いなだ	17
Yellow Jack	しまあじ	19
Lean Bluefin Tuna	あかみ	21
Medium Fatty Bluefin Tuna	ちゅうとろ	23
Fatty Bluefin Tuna	おおとろ	25
Juvenile Gizzard Shad	しんこ	27
Gizzard Shad	こはだ	29
Abalone	あわび	31
Japanese Horse Mackerel	あじ	33
Japanese Tiger Prawn	くるまえび	35
Cockle	とりがい	37
Red Clam	あかがい	39
Skipjack Tuna	かつお	41
Mantis Shrimp	しゃこ	43
Mackerel	さば	45
Octopus	たこ	47
Clam	はまぐり	49
Sardine	いわし	51
Halfbeak	さより	53
Sea Urchin	うに	55
Mactra Clam Muscle	こばしら	57
Salmon Roe	いくら	59
Conger Eel	あなご	61
Dried Calabash Gourd	かんぴょう巻き	63
Minced Prawn	おぼろ	65
Grilled Eggs	たまご	67

CHAPTER 2   How to Eat Sushi

INTRODUCTION Masuhiro Yamamoto   70

Use Your Hands   72
Use Chopsticks   74
Don't Spill the Topping   76
Use Soy Sauce   78
Eat Some Pickled Ginger   80
Drink Some Tea   81
Don't Dip Sushi Rice in Soy Sauce   82
Don't Use Soy Sauce with Tsume Sauce
Don't Turn the Sushi Upside Down   83
Don't Pull Off the Sushi Topping
Don't Bite the Sushi in Two   84
Don't Let the Sushi Sit

CHAPTER 3   Dining at Sukiyabashi Jiro

Reservations   88
Arriving at Sukiyabashi Jiro   89
Enjoying Our Omakase Tasting Menu   91
Dress Code   92
Payment
Visiting Sukiyabashi Jiro Again   95

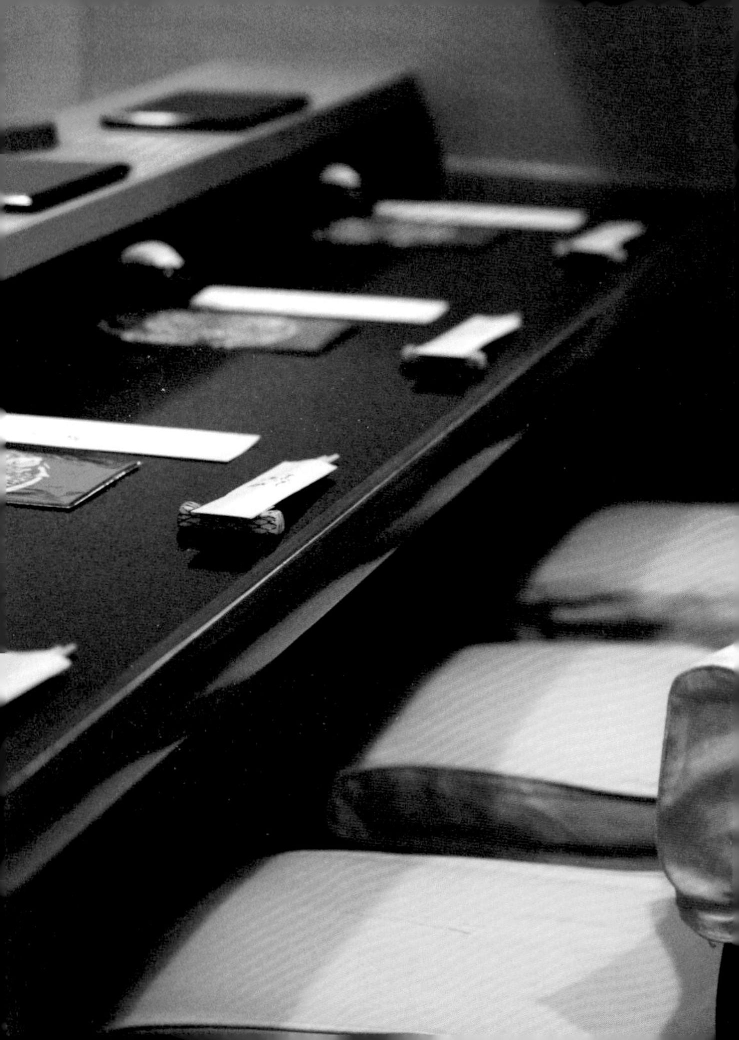

CHAPTER 1

Omakase Tasting Menu

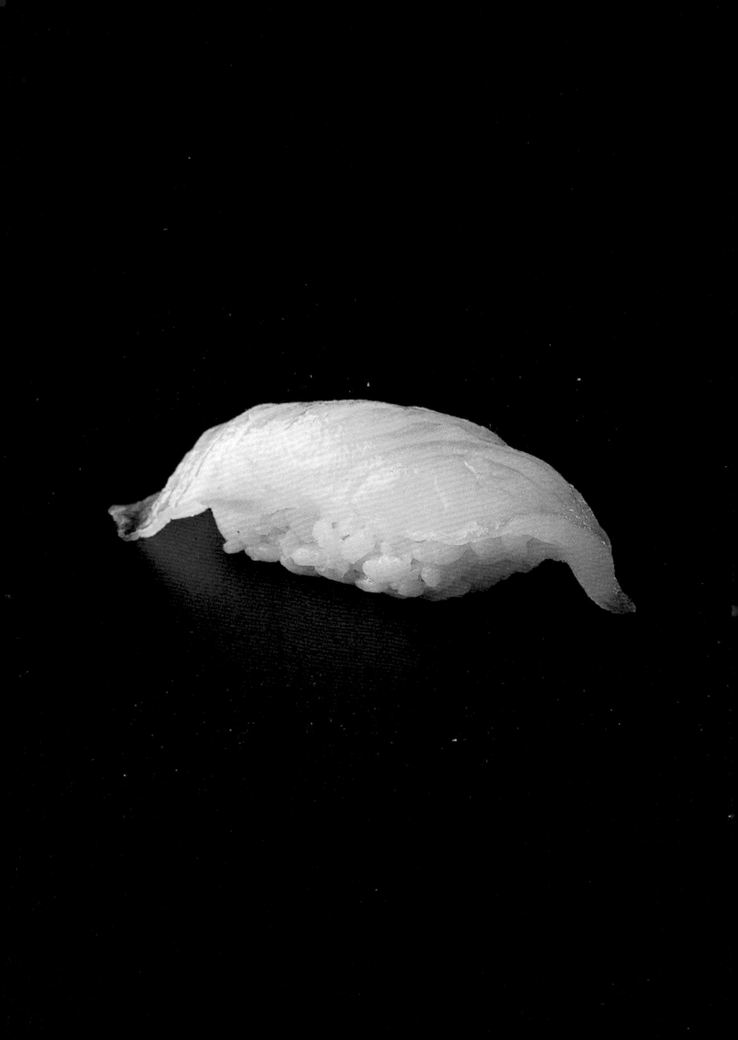

Sole

Karei かれい

SEASON April–October

Sukiyabashi Jiro was the first sushi restaurant to serve whitefish at the start of an omakase tasting menu. Jiro says, "We use marbled sole (*makogarei*). Because its flesh is tougher than that of a flounder's (*hirame*), we let it age for a longer time. If we buy sole from the market in the morning and have to serve it that day, we slice it very thinly. If we don't, it won't become one with the sushi rice. Since sole has a mild taste, we often serve it as the course starter. Many customers also order it as an encore."

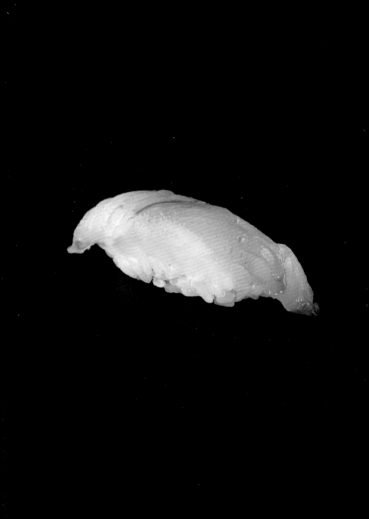

Flounder

Hirame　ひらめ

SEASON November–March

Along with sea bream (*tai*), flounder is the king of winter whitefish. At Sukiyabashi Jiro, we serve flounder as the first item of our omakase tasting menu. At Edo-style sushi restaurants, sushi chefs used to maintain the tradition of beginning the meal with tuna (*maguro*). This is because tuna is considered to be the epitome of Edo-style sushi. Mindful of the contrast between strong and mild flavors, at Sukiyabashi Jiro we serve milder-tasting flounder first, which was an innovative idea. Today, many sushi restaurants have followed in our footsteps by adopting this practice.

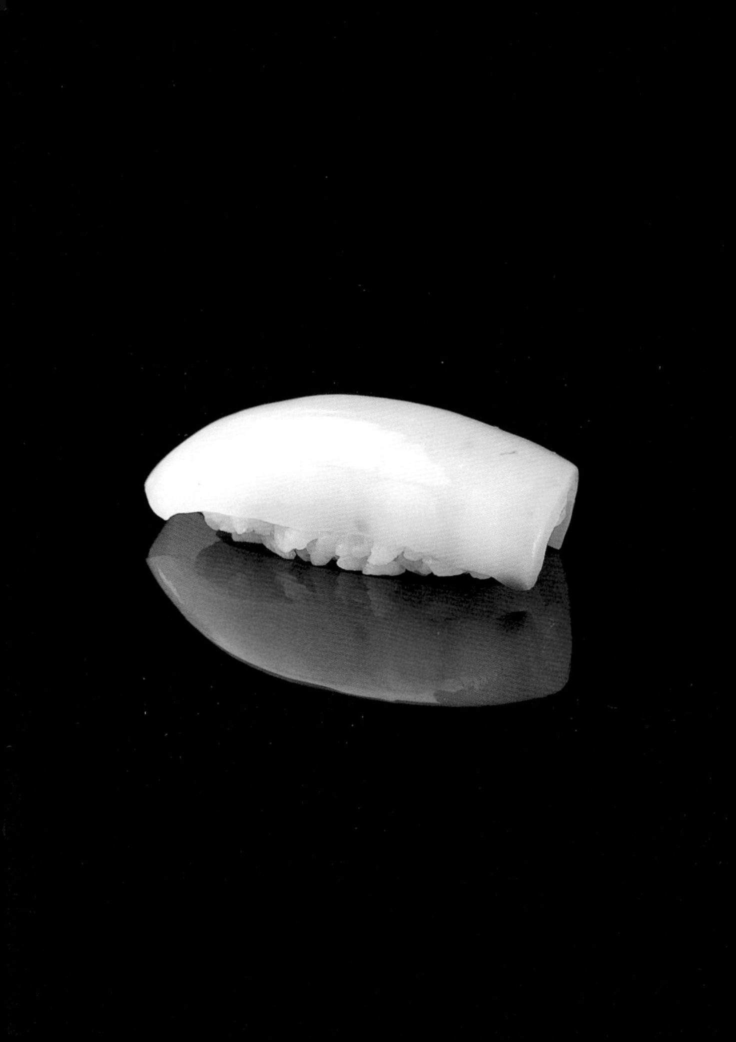

Juvenile Cuttlefish
Shin-Ika　しんいか

SEASON July–August

Cuttlefish (*sumi-ika*) in its juvenile state is called *shin-ika*. "Baby" is perhaps the more accurate term. Juvenile cuttlefish has smooth, glossy white skin. When you eat it as sushi, its silky texture on your tongue is pure pleasure. Jiro explains, "Unlike juvenile gizzard shad (*shinko*), juvenile cuttlefish is full of flavor no matter how small it is. It is delicious because it is so savory. Sushi topped with a piece of small but flavorful cuttlefish is the most delicious thing."

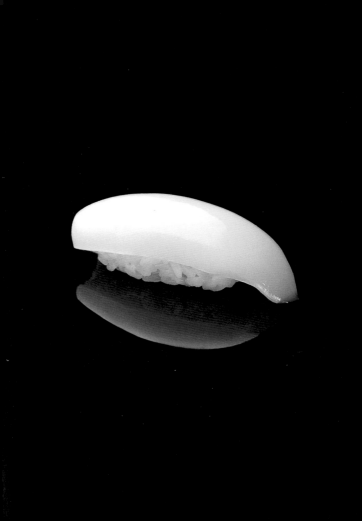

Golden Cuttlefish

Sumi-Ika すみいか

SEASON All seasons

At Sukiyabashi Jiro, the arrival of summer used to mean the appearance of bigfin reef squid (*aori-ika*) as a sushi topping. Nowadays, however, there are almost no opportunities for us to offer it due to its increasing rarity in fishing catches. So now we use golden cuttlefish. Jiro says, "A tempura restaurant that I frequent, Mikawa, used to serve a splendid tempura of bigfin reef squid, the likes of which I'd never seen before. But they are gone these days, and golden cuttlefish is offered instead. Golden cuttlefish has a skinny phase depending on the season, but it is still delicious all year round."

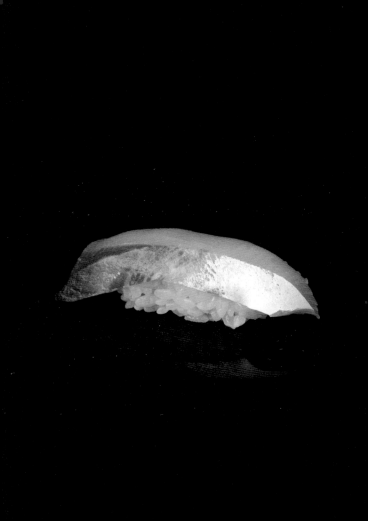

Juvenile Yellowtail

Inada いなだ

SEASON All seasons

Yellowtail (*buri*) is a species of amberjack. At Sukiyabashi Jiro, juvenile yellowtail makes its appearance as a "color" topping, third in order after the whitefish and cuttlefish courses. Jiro says, "In addition to juvenile yellowtail, yellow jack (*shima-aji*) and greater amberjack (*kanpachi*) can also be used as color toppings. These days, however, we turn to juvenile yellowtail most frequently. We began using it as a winter topping three years ago. We thought that it might be overpowered by other toppings, but because it is not as fatty as adult yellowtail, it has a clean, distinct flavor."

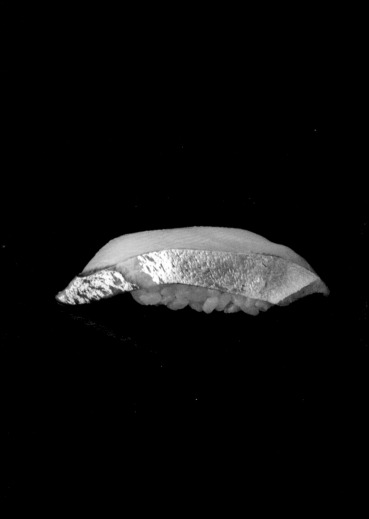

Yellow Jack

Shima-Aji しまあじ

SEASON Summer

At Sukiyabashi Jiro, we never use farmed or frozen fish.
So our yellow jack is, of course, wild caught. It has a fragrance
and taste that are completely different from those of farmed
yellow jack. Our customers go wide-eyed with amazement
when they catch the subtle aroma of the ocean in the fish
and bite into its firm flesh. Yellow jack is seldom found in fish
markets these days—only one or two may be available, if any.
However, when we are able to have some delivered chilled to
the restaurant with all its freshness and quality maintained,
it's outstanding. You are in for a treat if yellow jack makes an
appearance on a summer omakase tasting menu.

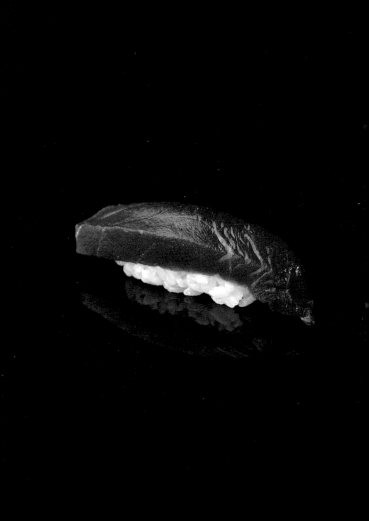

Lean Bluefin Tuna
Akami あかみ

SEASON All seasons

Akami is a lean cut of bluefin tuna (*maguro*). During the Edo era, over one hundred and fifty years ago, there was no refrigeration. Consequently, the fatty sections (*toro*) of tuna were not consumed but were removed and thrown away. Cuts of lean bluefin tuna were preserved by marinating them in casks of soy sauce. This technique is called *zuke*. At Sukiyabashi Jiro, we prepare bluefin tuna zuke for each of our reserved guests in advance. Jiro says, "The acidity of bluefin tuna and the savory flavor of soy sauce are a perfect match. Along with gizzard shad (*kohada*), it represents the pinnacle of Edo-style sushi."

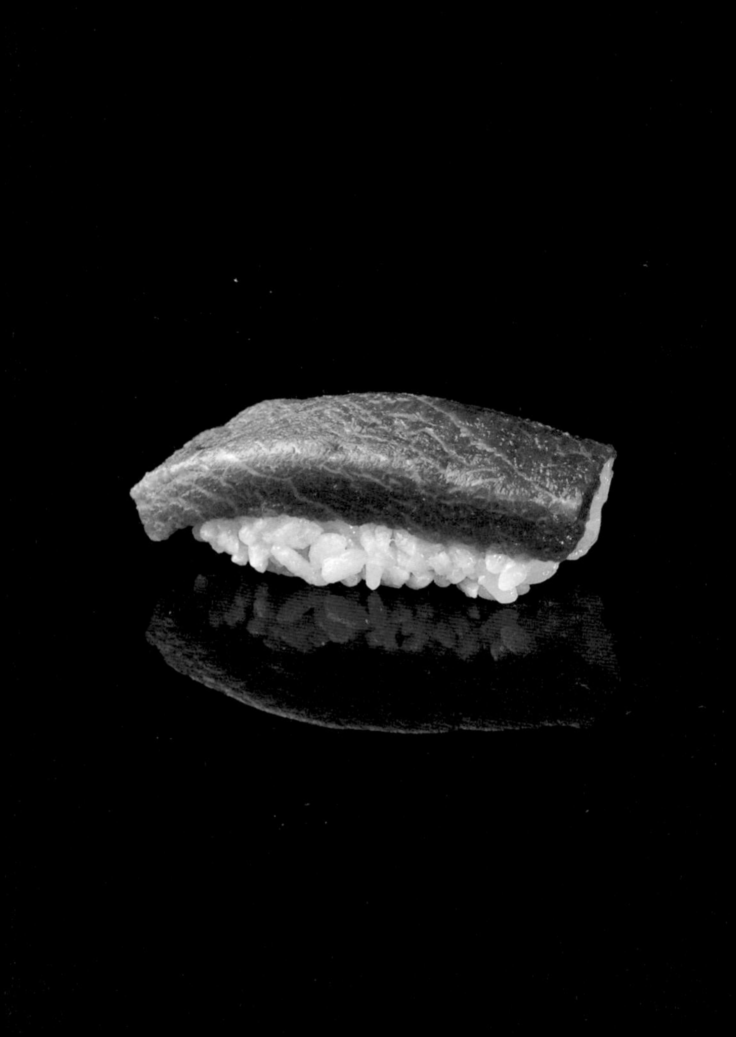

Medium Fatty Bluefin Tuna

Chutoro ちゅうとろ

SEASON All seasons

Jiro says, "Bluefin tuna cuts consist of the lean portion (*akami*), the medium fatty portion (*chutoro*), and the fatty portion (*otoro*). When it comes to umami, nothing beats medium fatty bluefin tuna. The moment you grasp the cut in your hand to make sushi, you can tell how fatty it is. Aging this cut takes skill. That's why it is essential to sample it every day." At Sukiyabashi Jiro, we of course use only fresh tuna. Jiro says, "A day without tuna means a day when a sushi restaurant can't open for business. Right now, it is the most important sushi topping."

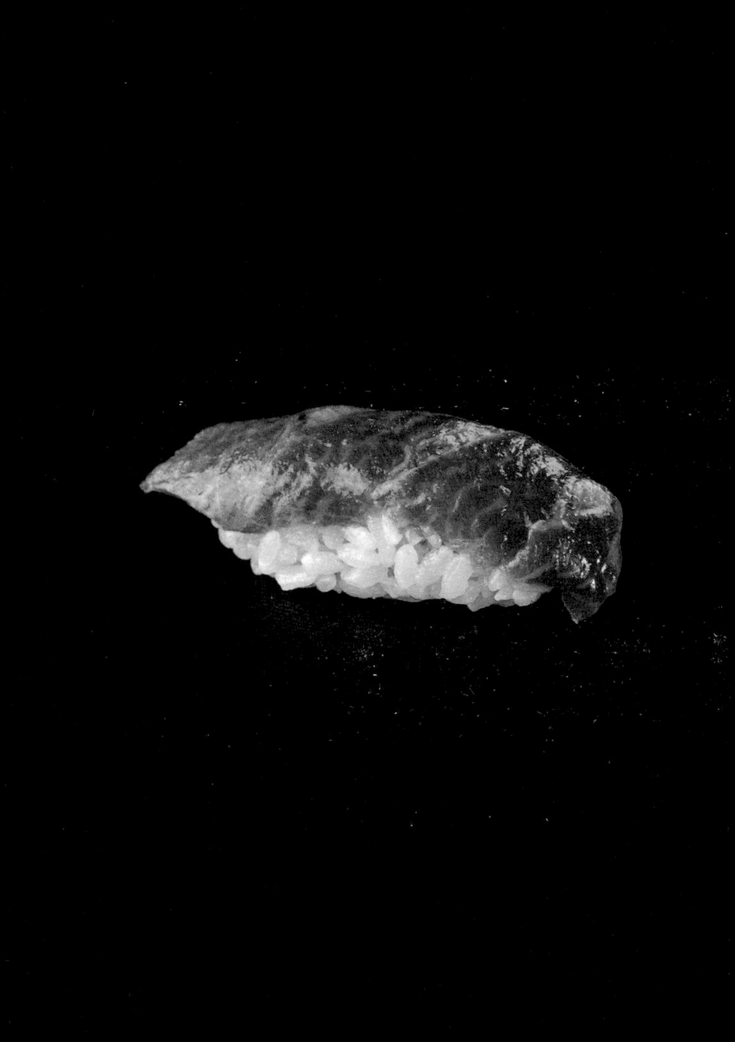

Fatty Bluefin Tuna

Otoro おおとろ

SEASON All seasons

———————————————

Sukiyabashi Jiro's tuna is procured from the Tsukiji Fish Market broker Fujita. For our fatty bluefin tuna, we want our fish to be fragrant, not simply fatty. This preference is also shared by Fujita. Jiro says, "There is no better feeling in the world than making sushi with good tuna. On the other hand, if we can't find good tuna, we feel quite uneasy. They say that good tuna comes from Oma, in Aomori Prefecture. But even in Oma, only one out of a hundred tuna meets our standards."

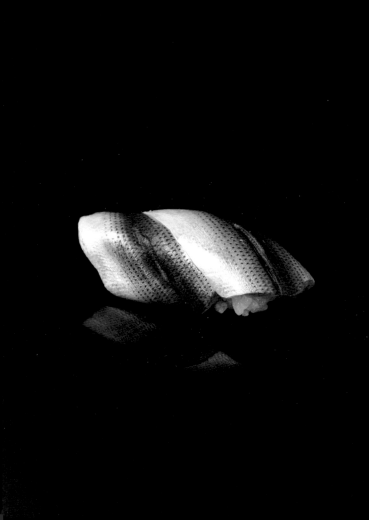

Juvenile Gizzard Shad

Shinko しんこ

SEASON End of July–August

In the past, juvenile gizzard shad held the starring role as the silver-skinned fish in season from fall to spring, as horse mackerel (*aji*) did from spring to summer. As delivery and refrigeration technologies advanced, gizzard shad and horse mackerel became available all year round. Jiro says, "We place two marinated juvenile gizzard shad pieces on sushi rice. You can taste the time and effort involved. Still, nothing beats it as a topping that offers the taste of summer."

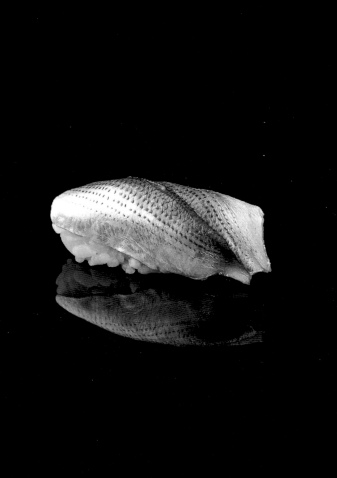

Gizzard Shad

Kohada　こはだ

SEASON　All seasons

When asked to name the most important sushi topping at
Sukiyabashi Jiro, Jiro immediately replies, "Gizzard shad."
He continues, "Gizzard shad makes or breaks a sushi chef.
Incredible flavor is created by marinating the pieces in vinegar.
But sometimes the shad may develop a heavy, oily odor during
this process, and if so, we must discard all of it. This is why it's
such a difficult fish to work with." At Sukiyabashi Jiro, we drape
one piece of gizzard shad diagonally over the sushi rice. Jiro says,
"I invented this style. It's an imitation of a feminine sitting pose."

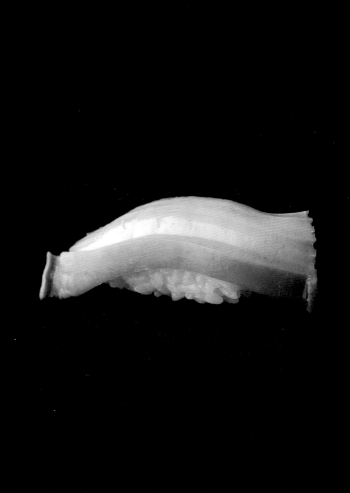

Abalone

Awabi あわび

SEASON May–September

Abalone is the king of summer shellfish. As a sushi topping, it is not served raw. At Sukiyabashi Jiro, we simmer it in sake and water for three to four hours, releasing the fragrance of the seashore without toughening the flesh. The abalone is then left to cool in its broth. Because abalone is difficult to handle when making sushi, we used to score it with a series of small cuts. High-quality abalone will release its scent simply upon being cut. Jiro says, "These days, however, we just warm the abalone when preparing sushi."

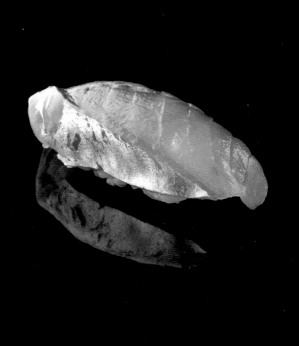

Japanese Horse Mackerel

Aji あじ

SEASON All seasons

Horse mackerel is served raw as sushi. But in the past, it was prepared by marinating it in salt and vinegar, a preparation called *sujime*. Jiro says, "When the catch is brought back from Tsukiji Market, the first fish I reach for are the horse mackerel. I immediately remove their innards, wash them in ice water, and place them in the refrigerator. This preserves the freshness of the fish and prevents a raw odor from forming." The flavor of Sukiyabashi Jiro's horse mackerel shines through even when it is served after tuna, a richly flavored fish. At the end of the omakase tasting menu, diners frequently ask for one more piece of horse mackerel; it is the most popularly requested encore item.

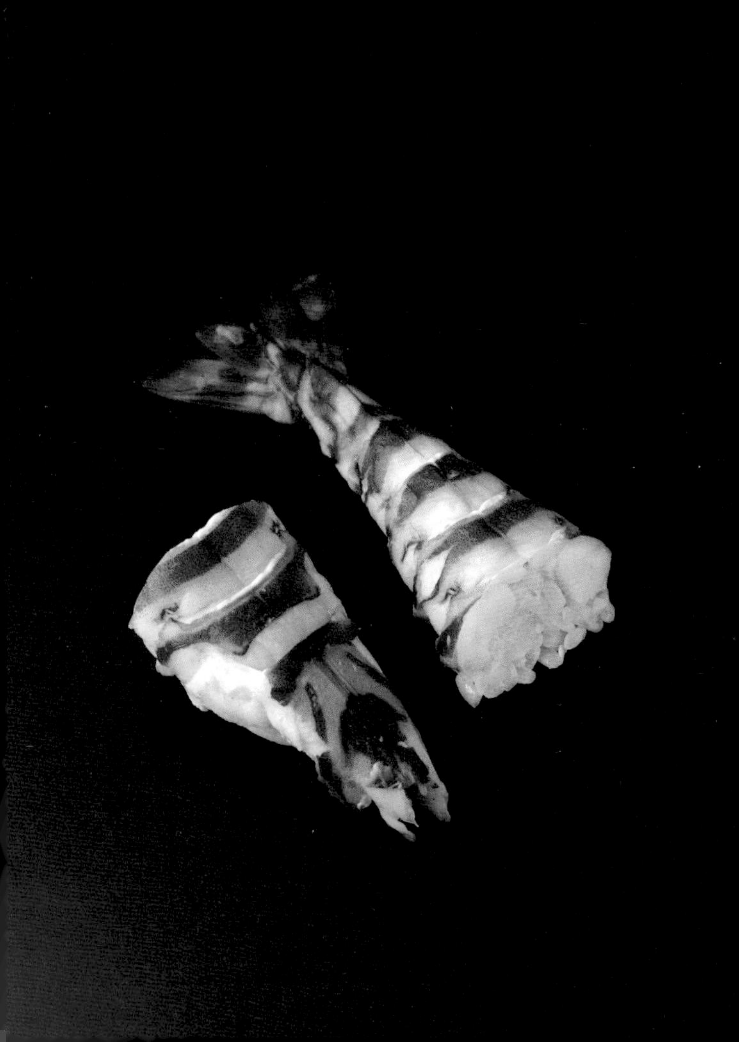

Japanese Tiger Prawn

Kuruma-Ebi くるまえび

SEASON All seasons

These days many sushi restaurants quickly parboil Japanese tiger prawns just before making them into sushi. Sukiyabashi Jiro originated this practice more than twenty-five years ago. Jiro says, "Tiger prawns are especially delicious in the summer. By cooking the prawns and letting them cool just a bit before using them in sushi, we allow their innards (*miso*) to be enjoyed by our customers. However, placing the prawns as a topping on sushi rice without the innards coming out is difficult. Because they have a high water content, they can slip out of our hands."

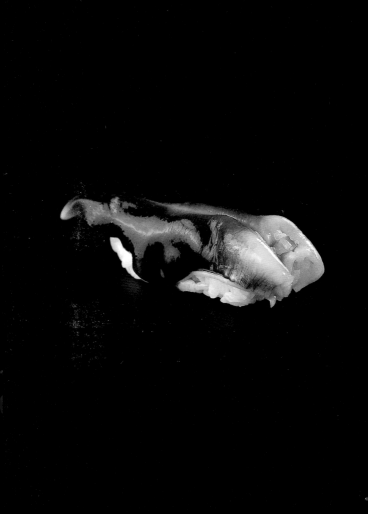

Cockle

Torigai とりがい

SEASON April–May

The return of cockles announces the arrival of spring. It is a strictly seasonal bivalve mollusk that disappears the moment summer starts. Jiro says, "A long time ago, you could find endless amounts of excellent cockles in Tokyo Bay. The type of cockle we use now has a different luster and size. Even though it is large and thick, it is still soft and very sweet. Because cockle is a sushi topping that embodies the taste of a season, it is an absolutely essential shellfish for our springtime omakase tasting menu."

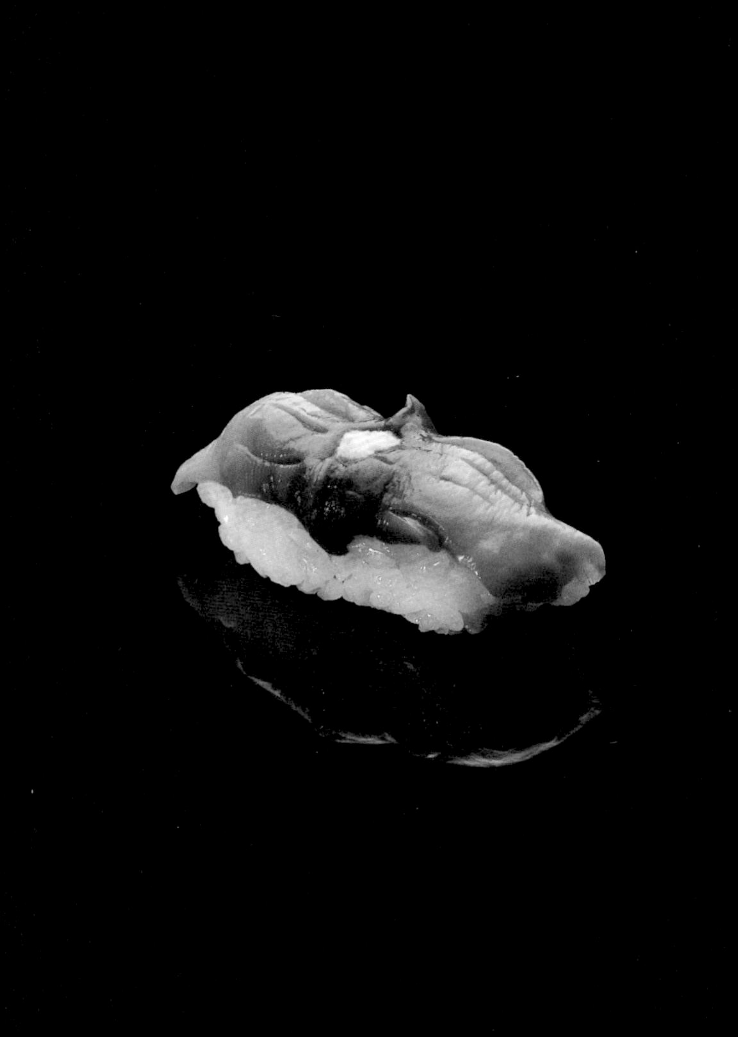

Red Clam
Akagai あかがい

SEASON All seasons

After the Second World War, red clams could no longer be found in Tokyo Bay. Subsequently, the highest-quality red clams in Japan came from Yuriage in Miyagi Prefecture. The region's clams were wiped out by the 2011 Tohoku earthquake and tsunami, however, and now they are sourced from Oita and Kagawa Prefectures instead. Jiro says, "Red clams are notoriously difficult shellfish to use. You can't tell what their quality will be until you shuck them. Like shrimp and crab, shellfish must be fresh above all else. At Sukiyabashi Jiro, we serve red clam straight out of its shell."

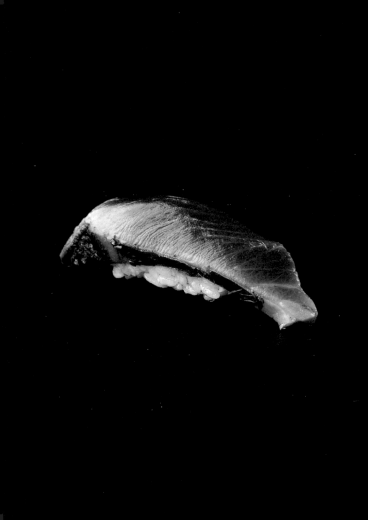

Skipjack Tuna

Katsuo かつお

SEASON June–November

Skipjack tuna is a vexing fish. At first glance, it's hard to know if you've caught a good fish or a bad one. It is only after you fillet it that you can tell how fatty it is. At Sukiyabashi Jiro, we roast three fillets over burning straw, which allows us to lightly grill the skin without cooking the flesh. The fish is then immediately placed in the freezer. Jiro says, "If grilled skipjack tuna is cooled in cold water, the precious fat between the skin and the flesh flows away. Sushi made with skipjack tuna smoked over straw is fragrant and rich in savory flavor. It is popular with our international guests."

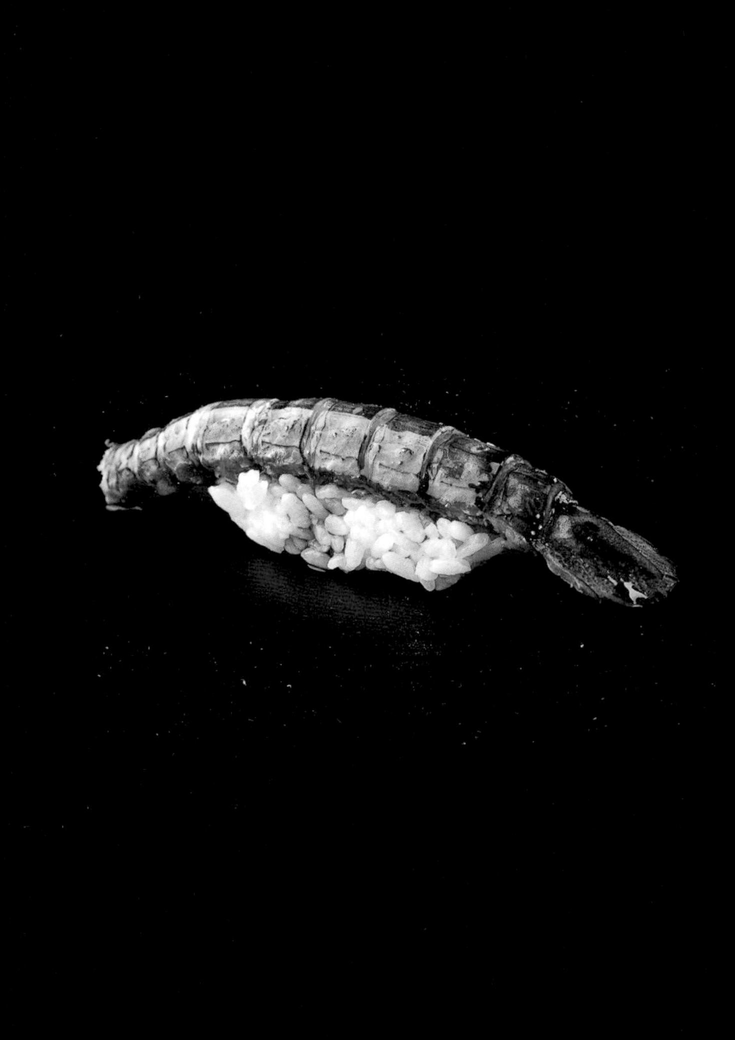

Mantis Shrimp

Shako しゃこ

SEASON June–October

At Sukiyabashi Jiro, mantis shrimp makes its appearance immediately after skipjack tuna. Because we smoke our skipjack tuna over burning straw, it has a lingering aftertaste. While a pronounced flavor is generally to be desired, it can interfere with the taste of the next piece of sushi. Roe-bearing mantis shrimp, cooked and then steeped in broth, is an effective palate cleanser. At the same time, its rich flavor blooms in your mouth. If the serving order of the skipjack tuna and mantis shrimp were reversed, both flavors would be wasted. Served in the correct order, they make a heavenly match in the early summer.

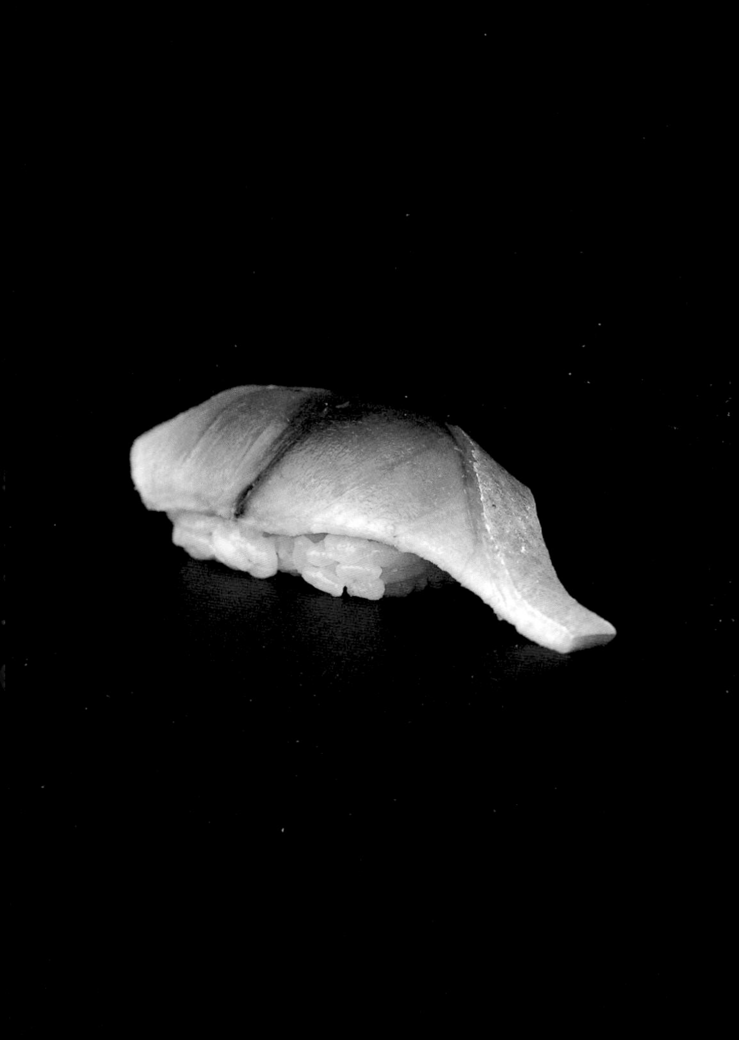

Mackerel

Saba さば

SEASON November–March

Sitting at the counter of Sukiyabashi Jiro, Heston Blumenthal, the owner-chef of The Fat Duck in London, said, "Saba is my favorite food in the world." As he bit into the wonderfully savory vinegared mackerel sushi, he was at a loss for words. Jiro says, "If vinegared mackerel is not properly prepared, the fish's rich flavor is not fully expressed. We actually marinate our mackerel in vinegar for about a week. This delectable fish is highly popular with our international customers."

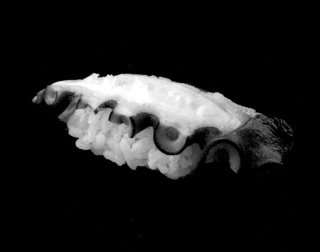

Octopus

Tako たこ

SEASON January–February

Other sushi restaurants serve octopus year-round. At Sukiyabashi Jiro, however, it makes its appearance in midwinter. Joël Robuchon, the French master chef, said, "Whenever I'm eating octopus, it feels like I'm chewing rubber. It doesn't taste good, and I have a hard time with it." But the moment he tried Sukiyabashi Jiro's octopus, he exclaimed, "It tastes like lobster!" When preparing octopus, we knead its flesh for one hour, which releases its fragrance and flavor. It then tastes as if its diet had consisted purely of crustaceans like shrimp and lobster. At present, octopus is Sukiyabashi Jiro's winter specialty.

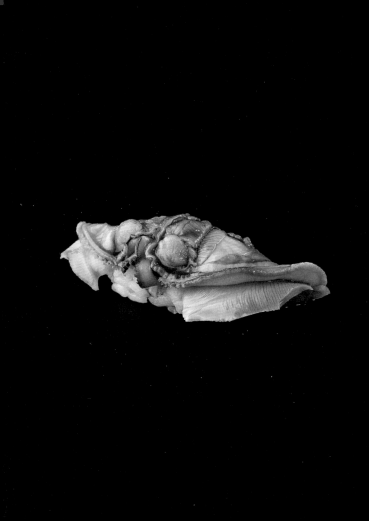

Clam

Hamaguri はまぐり

SEASON November–March

Clams are bivalve mollusks inhabiting the shoals of the sea. Since the Edo era, clams have been found in great abundance in Tokyo Bay. Thus, like tuna, gizzard shad, and conger eel (*anago*), it is a part of classic Edo-style sushi. Jiro says, "Because clams can quickly turn tough when cooked, we keep them on the fire for just a short time. We then steep them in broth, to which we add seasonings like sugar and soy sauce to adjust the flavor."

A sweet, juicy clam is a perfect match for sushi rice.

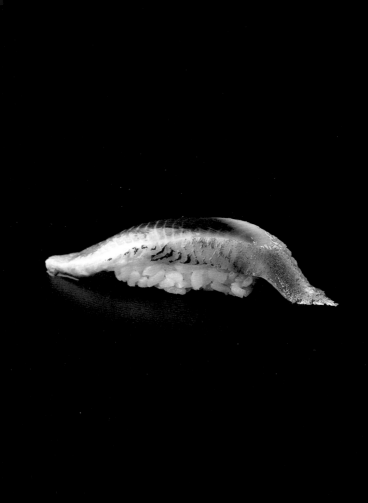

Sardine

Iwashi いわし

SEASON June–October

———————————

The sardine has been regarded as a cheap fish. At Sukiyabashi Jiro, however, it comes after tuna or prawn in our omakase tasting menu. Jiro says, "Sardines grow fatty in summer and rival tuna in richness. Because they spoil quickly, we prepare them immediately when they are brought in from Tsukiji Fish Market. We hold them under ice water as we remove their innards in order to minimize their deterioration. Working quickly is crucial. Please eat sardine sushi as soon as it is served. If you leave it sitting, it will quickly develop an unpleasant odor."

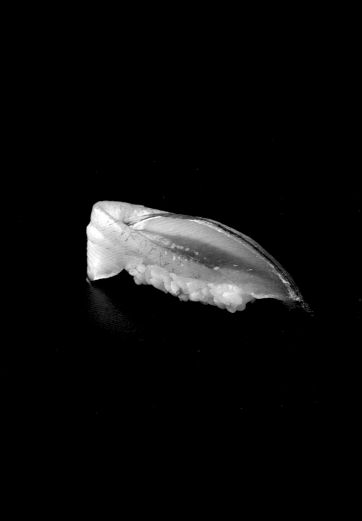

Halfbeak

Sayori さより

SEASON November–March

For sushi chefs, halfbeak is not considered a whitefish but rather a silver-skinned fish. It has a clear flavor, and thanks to its fattiness, it glides over the tongue. Jiro says, "As its old nickname 'needlefish' suggests, halfbeak is a long, thin fish. We would twist two together and place them on top of the sushi rice. Recently there have been many plump halfbeak, so we can't twist them anymore." For a while, halfbeak was served frequently because sardine catches were poor. However, because sardines are abundant again, the opportunity for halfbeak to appear on the menu has become limited.

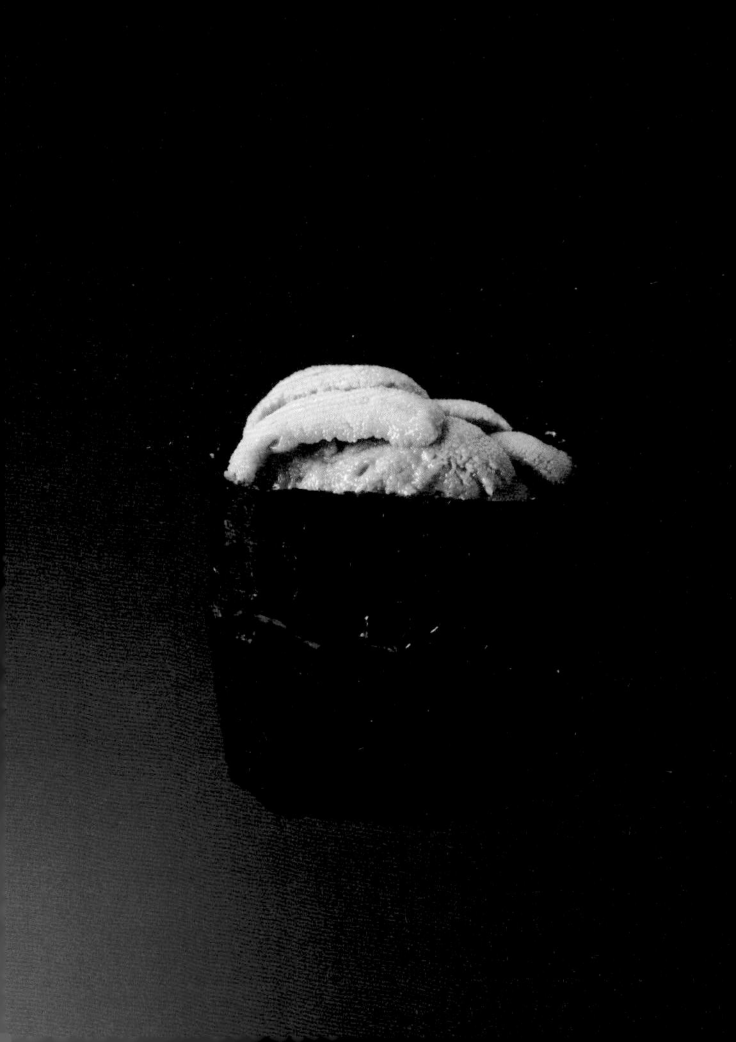

Sea Urchin

Uni うに

SEASON All seasons

When he placed a piece of Sukiyabashi Jiro's sea urchin sushi in his mouth, the French maestro Joël Robuchon observed, "It's as if I'm eating cream." Sukiyabashi Jiro sources sea urchin grown off the northern island of Hokkaido. We roll the sushi using nori seaweed that we grill over coals every morning, a practice that sets Sukiyabashi Jiro apart from other sushi restaurants. Jiro says, "I put just enough sea urchin on the rice so that when you place the entire sushi piece in your mouth, the flavors of the sea urchin and nori and sushi rice balance each other and become one."

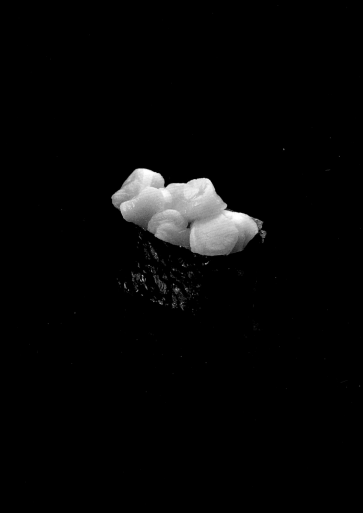

Mactra Clam Muscle
Kobashira こばしら

SEASON All seasons

_____

This piece of shellfish is actually the adductor muscle of a
mactra clam. At Sukiyabashi Jiro, our version differs from
what is typically offered by other sushi restaurants in one
major respect: its enormous size. Mactra clam muscle makes
its appearance in the latter half of our omakase tasting menu,
served in a "battleship roll" after the sea urchin and salmon
roe courses. Jiro says, "We roast our nori seaweed every
morning. Mactra clam muscles match its flavor perfectly.
These days, however, it's been tough getting our hands on
large ones. These clams may disappear entirely in the near
future, so be sure to try the sushi soon and savor its taste."

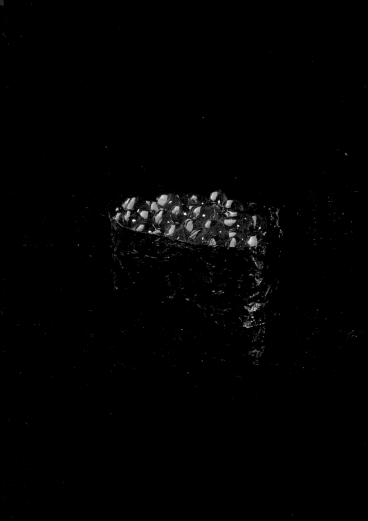

Salmon Roe

Ikura いくら

SEASON All seasons

At Sukiyabashi Jiro, the only type of fish we buy is the kind that makes good sushi: fresh fish delivered chilled from Tsukiji Market with its freshness and flavor intact. We never use farmed or frozen fish. However, there is one exception to this rule: salmon roe. Jiro says, "Salmon produce roe only once a year, in the fall. Because of this, we decided to use frozen salmon roe so we could serve it year-round. We marinate the roe in soy sauce. It has a smooth texture and mild taste on par with fresh chicken eggs. I'm very happy when customers tell me that our salmon roe sushi tastes like raw egg over rice."

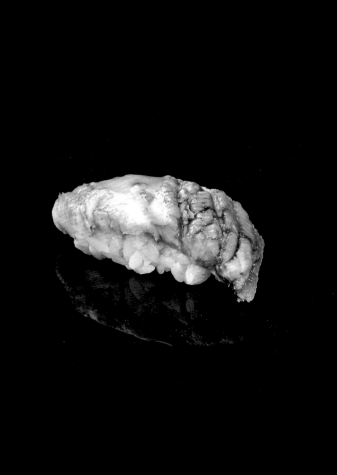

Conger Eel

Anago あなご

SEASON All seasons

Jiro says, "Because we cook our conger eel until it is very tender, serving it as sushi is very difficult. It is perhaps the most difficult sushi to prepare. When shaping the sushi piece, you can't exert any pressure on the eel." Jiro laughs. "Even if it looks like we're handling it firmly, we're actually just barely touching it." At Sukiyabashi Jiro, our conger eel is perfectly finished just by simmering it. Unlike other sushi restaurants, we don't broil it as well before making it into sushi.

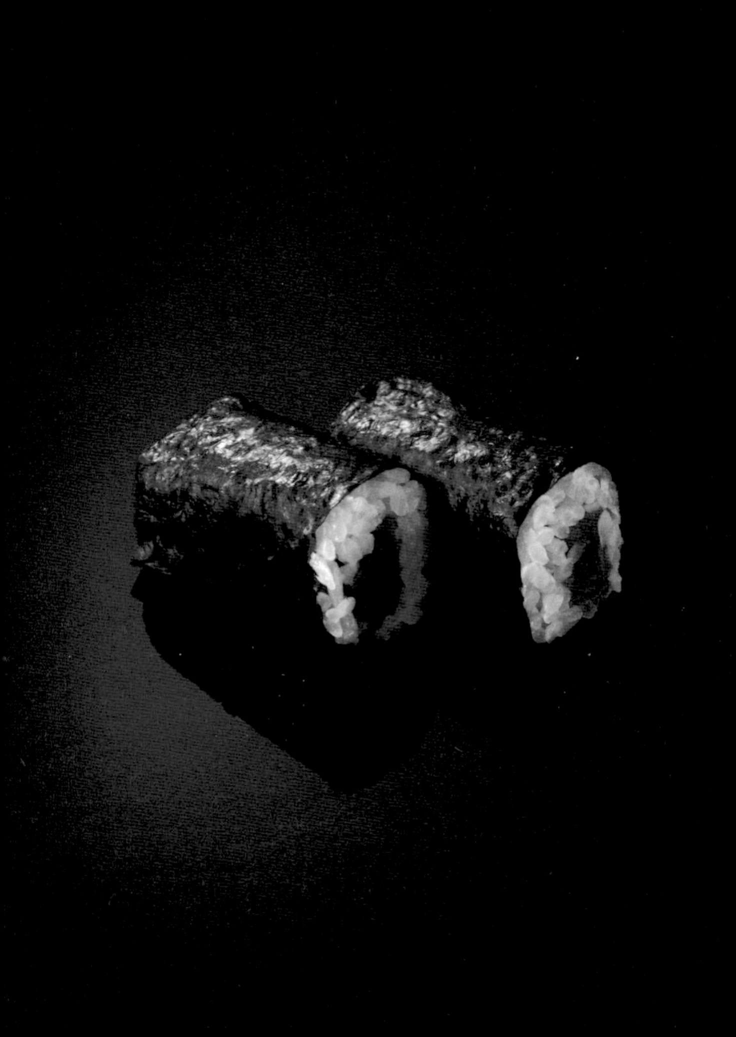

Dried Calabash Gourd
Kanpyo Maki かんぴょう巻き

SEASON All seasons

Sukiyabashi Jiro's sushi rolls (*maki*) made out of simmered dried calabash gourd shavings are not part of the omakase tasting menu, but we serve it after the conger eel course upon the customer's request. Jiro says, "In the past, we used to prepare this roll, but almost no one ordered it. We continued to recommend it, however, and it gradually became popular. Now we make it all day long. I wouldn't be surprised if we make the most dried gourd rolls in Japan. It's unfortunate that you can't get gourds now as good as the ones in the past."

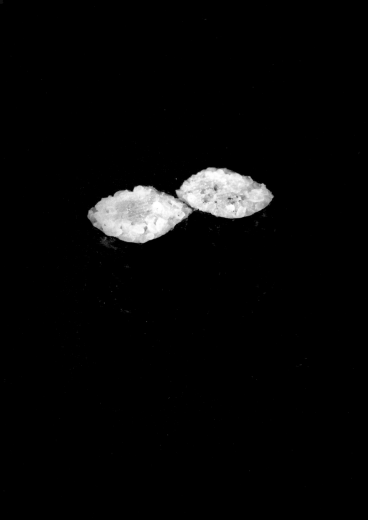

Minced Prawn

Oboro おぼろ

SEASON All seasons

This is an essential topping for *chirashi* sushi, a colorful dish of seafood, vegetables, and egg served over a bowl of vinegared rice. However, because we currently do not offer chirashi sushi at Sukiyabashi Jiro, we make sushi rolls filled with *oboro* upon request. Our oboro is made exclusively from minced prawn. Jiro says, "Oboro is delicious if you take the time to make it."

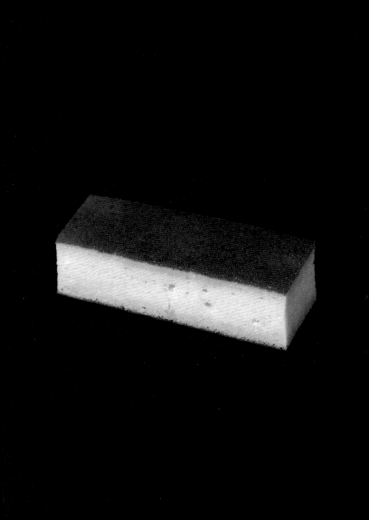

Grilled Eggs

Tamago たまご

SEASON All seasons

Referred to as a "rolled omelet" by some of our international customers, *tamago* is the final offering in our omakase tasting menu. Jiro says, "At Sukiyabashi Jiro, we consider the ability to make a good tamago the sign of a professional chef. In addition to eggs, we usually mix in grated Japanese yam (*yamato imo*) and shrimp. Making just one tamago takes about an hour. In the past we used to serve it on top of rice as sushi. But since our customers have by that point already enjoyed many types of sushi as part of our omakase, we now serve tamago simply by itself, like a dessert."

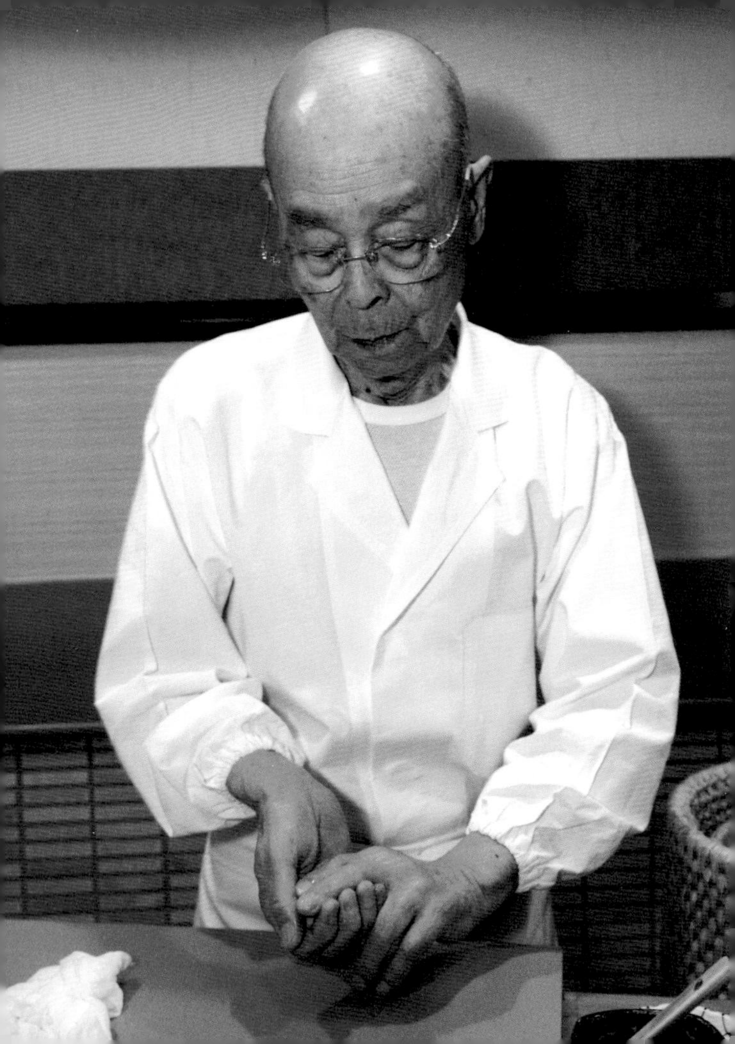

CHAPTER 2

How to Eat Sushi

INTRODUCTION

It doesn't matter if you pick up sushi with your fingers or with chopsticks. At Sukiyabashi Jiro, the chopsticks are tapered at both ends. This type of chopstick is called *rikyubashi*. It is said that when you use one end, God uses the other. The chopsticks' length is 7 *sun* 5 *bu*, or roughly 23 centimeters. It is about the length from one's elbow to wrist, and this served as a traditional unit of measure when it was developed in the Edo era. Two of these units make 1 *shaku* 5 *sun*, which is the length of chopsticks used to cook tempura. Tempura chopsticks are made of bamboo. That is why the kanji character for "chopsticks," or *hashi* (箸), is written using the character for "person" (者) under the character for "bamboo" (竹). The sushi or tempura chef and the customer face each other with a distance of three shaku in between. This is just the right distance for serving freshly made sushi or fried tempura. The distance also promotes a congenial atmosphere between the chef and the customer without being smothering. This finely tuned distance lies at the foundation of cuisine originating from Edo-era food stalls. At a sushi or tempura counter, there is no need to trade banter while drinking or dining together; in fact, it is taboo. If you wish to chat and enjoy conversation, please sit at a table.

Masuhiro Yamamoto

1 Use Your Hands

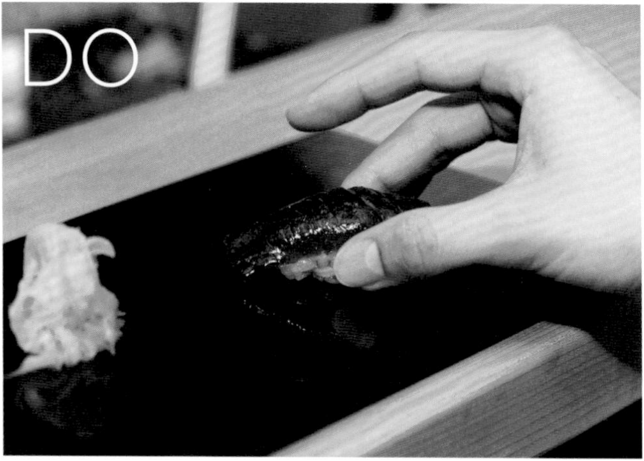
DO

Because good sushi is made with an extremely light touch, the rice is airy, not solid. When the piece is placed on your plate, it lands softly. It is not easy to hold. Gently lift it up by the sides so that it maintains its shape.

DON'T

Do not pick up the sushi by its ends; it is likely to fall apart.

2 Use Chopsticks

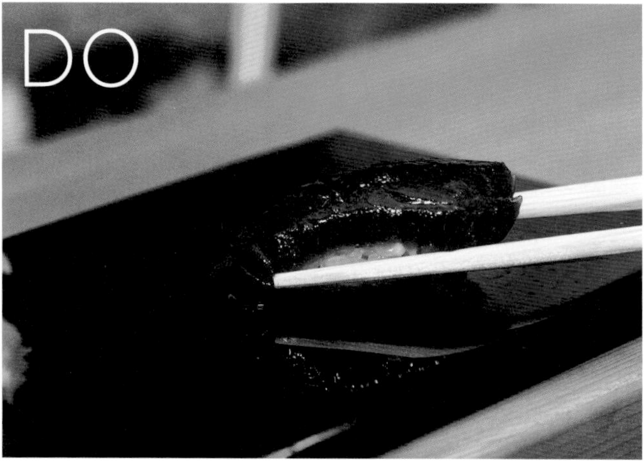
DO

If you prefer to use chopsticks to eat sushi, think of the sushi piece as a little portable shrine. Hold your chopsticks parallel to the plate, as if they were the shrine's carrying poles, and lift the sushi up gently by its sides.

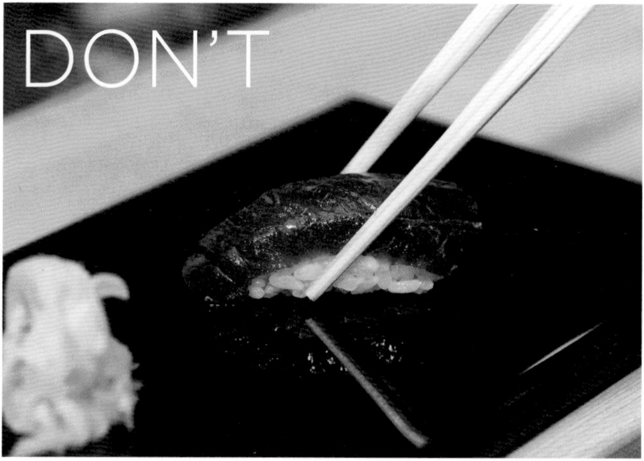
DON'T

Do not try to pick up the sushi piece through the middle, with your chopsticks held vertical to the plate. It will definitely fall apart.

3 Don't Spill the Topping

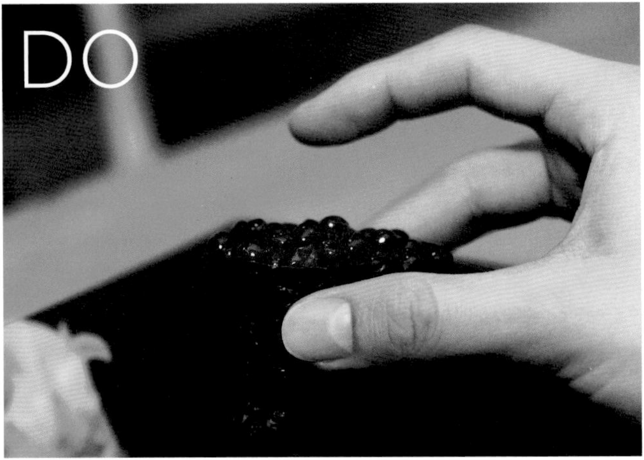
DO

When eating a battleship roll, whether using your hands or chopsticks, pick the sushi up gently by its sides and put the entire piece in your mouth.

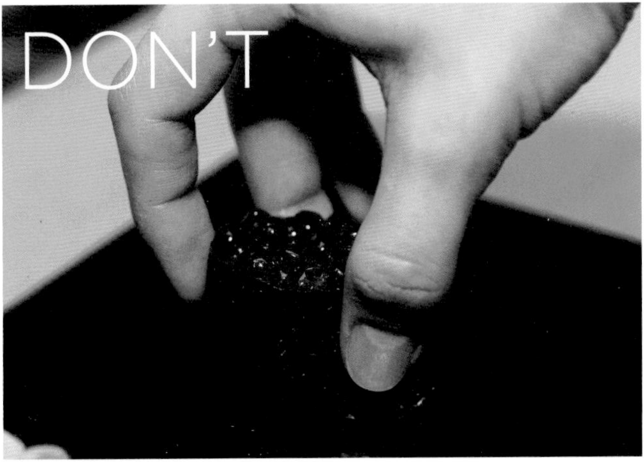
DON'T

Do not pick up the sushi from above, as the topping will fall out when you lift it to your mouth, and do not attempt to bite the piece.

4 Use Soy Sauce

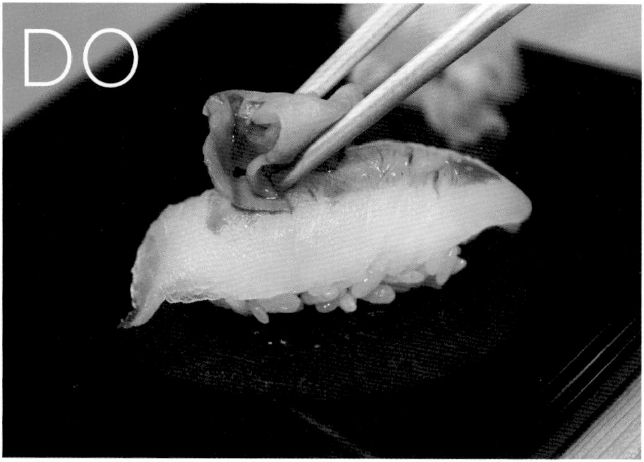
DO

If, by chance, the sushi chef has neglected to brush nikiri soy sauce on your sushi, pick up a small amount of pickled ginger (*shoga*), dip it in soy sauce, and use it like a paintbrush on top of the sushi.

DON'T

Do not pick up the sushi piece and dip it directly into the soy sauce.

5 Eat Some Pickled Ginger

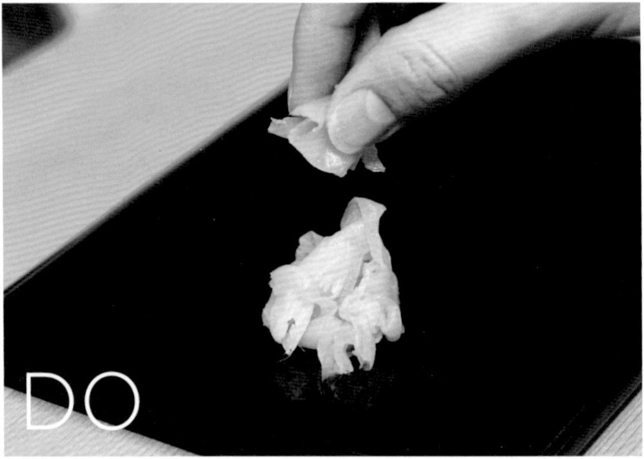
DO

Pickled ginger acts as a palate cleanser. However, too much of it will burn your taste buds. Eat just a pinch of it to remove any aftertaste between courses.

6 Drink Some Tea

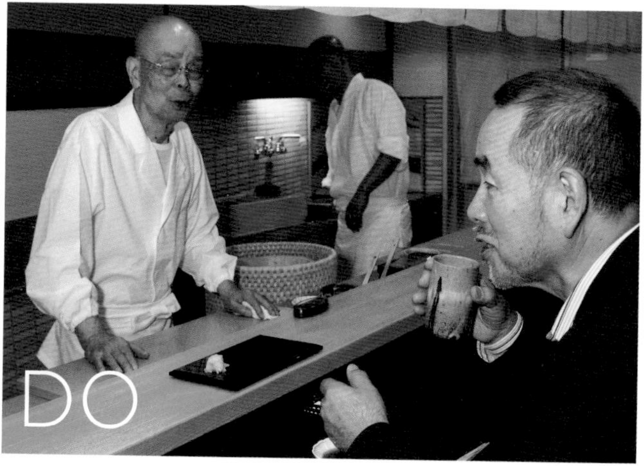
DO

Jiro believes that drinking tea is the best way to cleanse the palate. Water is also available for guests who would prefer a cool beverage.

7 Don't Dip Sushi Rice in Soy Sauce

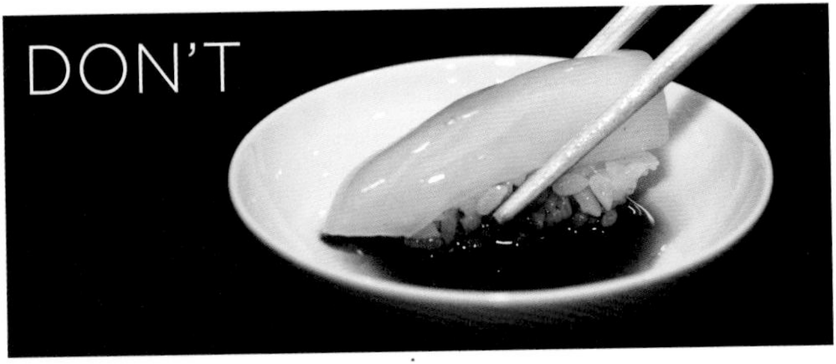
DON'T

By doing so you will spoil its flavor, and the piece will fall apart.

8 Don't Use Soy Sauce with Tsume Sauce

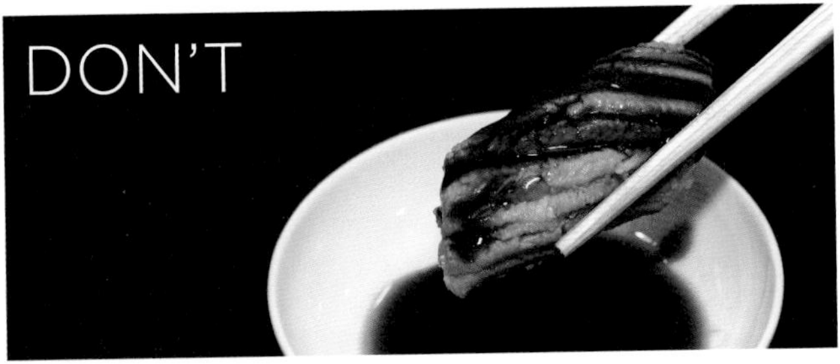
DON'T

Sushi pieces made with sweet tsume sauce brushed on top do not require any other flavoring.

9 Don't Turn the Sushi Upside Down

If you eat a sushi piece upside down, the sensation of the rice hitting your palate instead of your tongue will create a strange mouthfeel.

10 Don't Pull Off the Sushi Topping

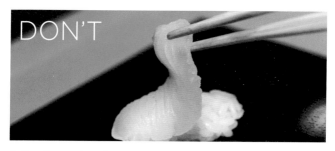

Pulling the topping off a piece of sushi is a great insult to the sushi chef.

11 Don't Bite the Sushi in Two

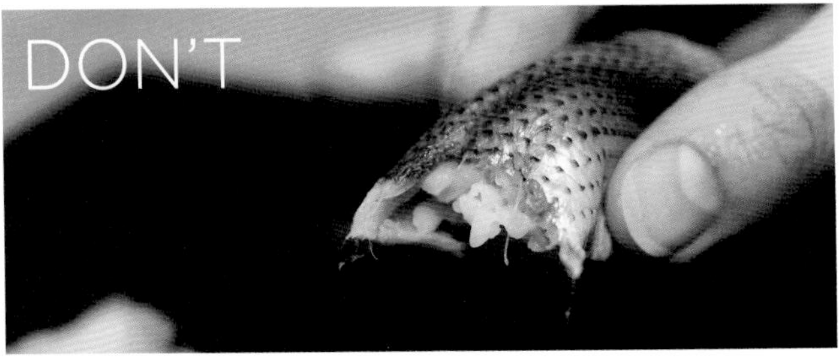
DON'T

A piece of sushi should be roughly six centimeters or two inches long, a size that allows it to fit into your mouth whole.

12 Don't Let the Sushi Sit

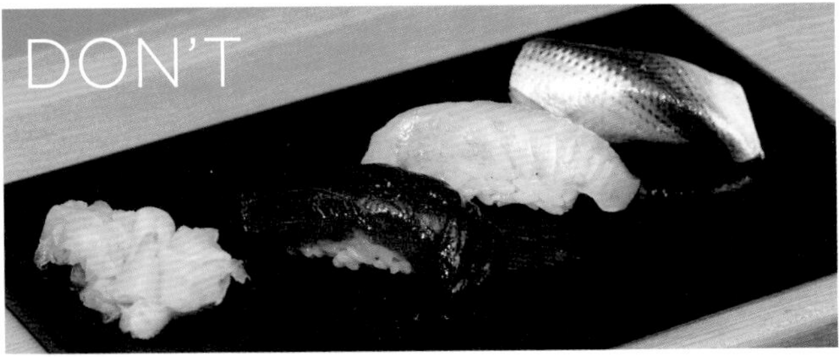
DON'T

There is nothing more delicious than a fresh piece of sushi that has just been served to you.

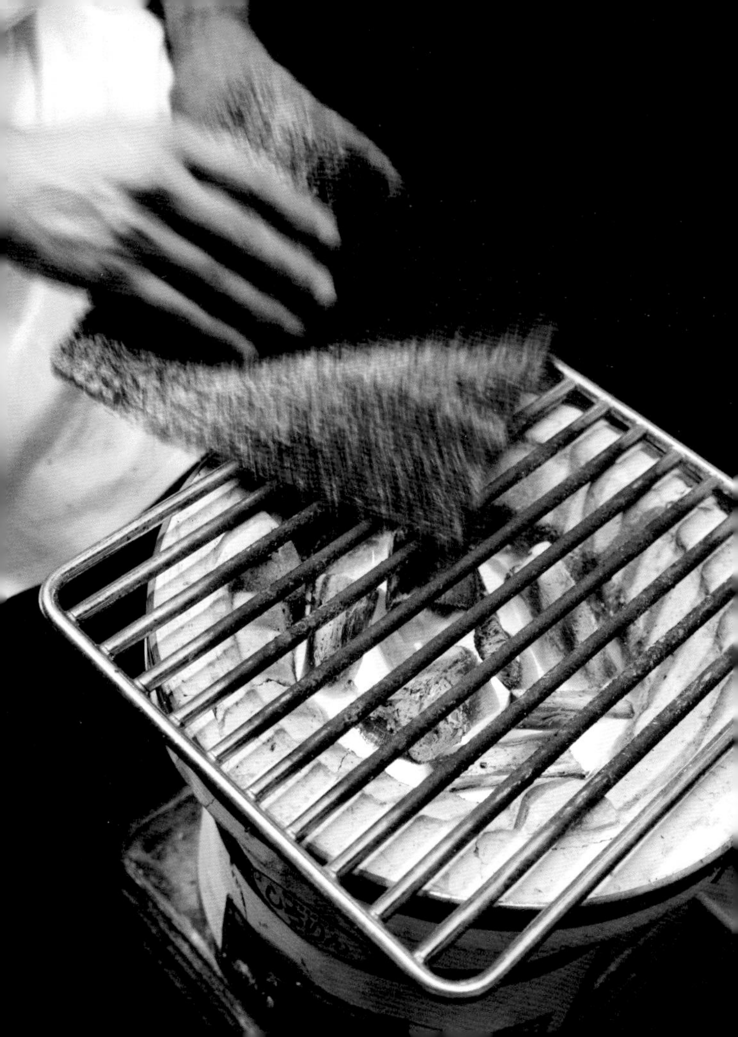

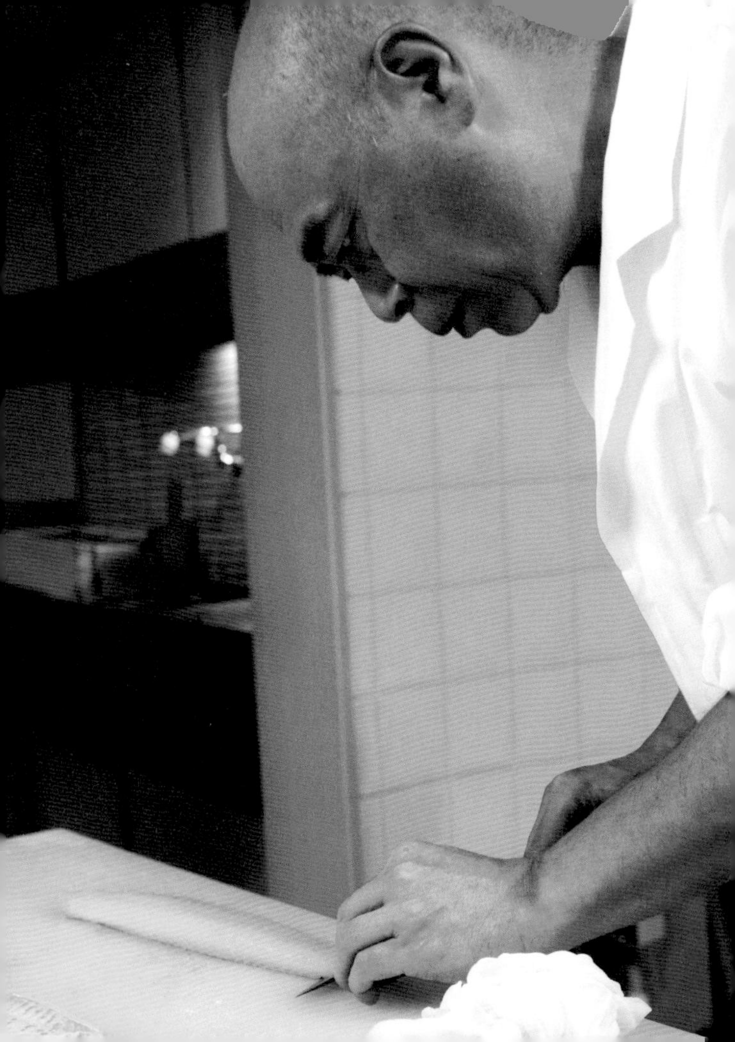

CHAPTER 3

Dining at Sukiyabashi Jiro

Reservations

Sukiyabashi Jiro accepts reservations starting at 9 a.m. on the first day of the month, with the exceptions of Sundays and the month of January. Many of our international guests ask their hotel's concierge to make reservations for them. Regrettably, we cannot answer phone calls in languages other than Japanese. We welcome single diners. However, Jiro serves sushi at a quick pace, and many single diners cannot keep up. To fully enjoy sushi at Sukiyabashi Jiro, we recommend a party of two or more guests.

Arriving at Sukiyabashi Jiro

Please observe the reservation time and try not to be late. Because we cook and prepare our sushi rice based on your reservation time, if you are late, you won't be able to enjoy Sukiyabashi Jiro's sushi to its full extent. The restaurant has only ten counter seats. Since the seafood that we procure daily from Tsukiji Market is selected to best complement the taste of sushi rice, we do not prepare appetizers. We also do not serve sake. Jiro's recommended beverage to accompany sushi is green tea. The best way to enjoy Jiro's sushi is to concentrate on the dining experience. Therefore, we ask that you please refrain from taking photos of the sushi. Instead, when you leave, we would be pleased to take a commemorative photograph for you at the entrance, if you wish.

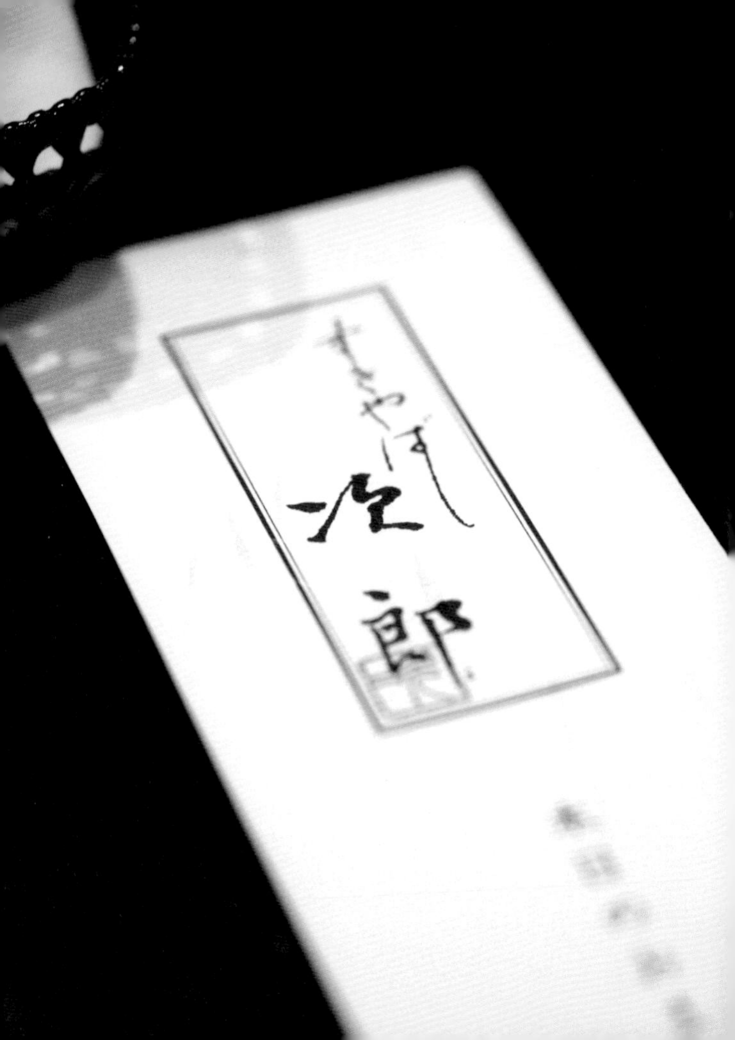
すきやばし
次郎

Enjoying Our Omakase Tasting Menu

At Sukiyabashi Jiro, we currently serve only the omakase tasting menu. Jiro makes the sushi for all customers. The tasting menu served at the counter is created in the morning each day, and the courses are served in order. The full menu consists of about twenty pieces of sushi. That is quite a large amount. However, Jiro takes care to make each piece smaller for older women customers. Please eat the sushi soon after it is placed on the plate in front of you. The flavors are at their most exquisite when the sushi has just been prepared. Because nikiri soy sauce has already been brushed on the sushi, there is no need to dip it in a saucer of soy sauce.

Dress Code

Sukiyabashi Jiro has no special dress code. Many of our male guests wear jackets or blazers. We may, however, refuse service to customers wearing T-shirts, shorts, or sandals. We ask that our guests refrain from wearing strong perfume or cologne. Please hand us your bag to store for safekeeping instead of slinging it over the back of your chair.

Payment

In the past, we accepted only cash, but now you can pay by credit card as well. The cost of the omakase tasting menu is 30,000 yen plus tax for either lunch or dinner.

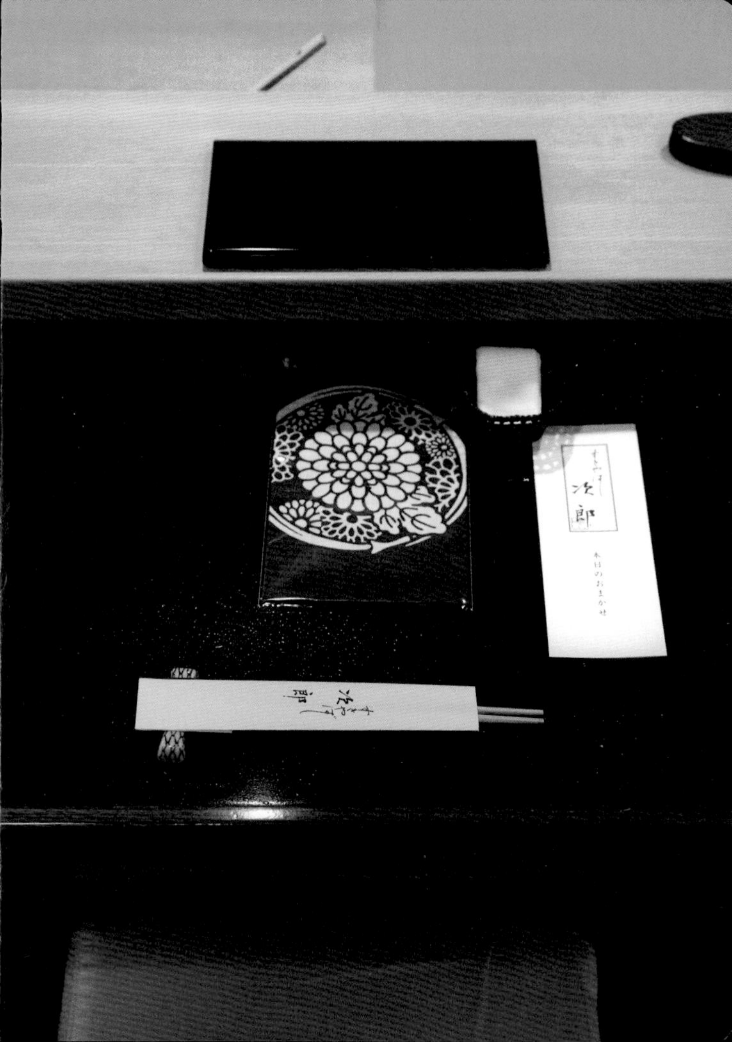
すきやばし
次郎
本日のおまかせ

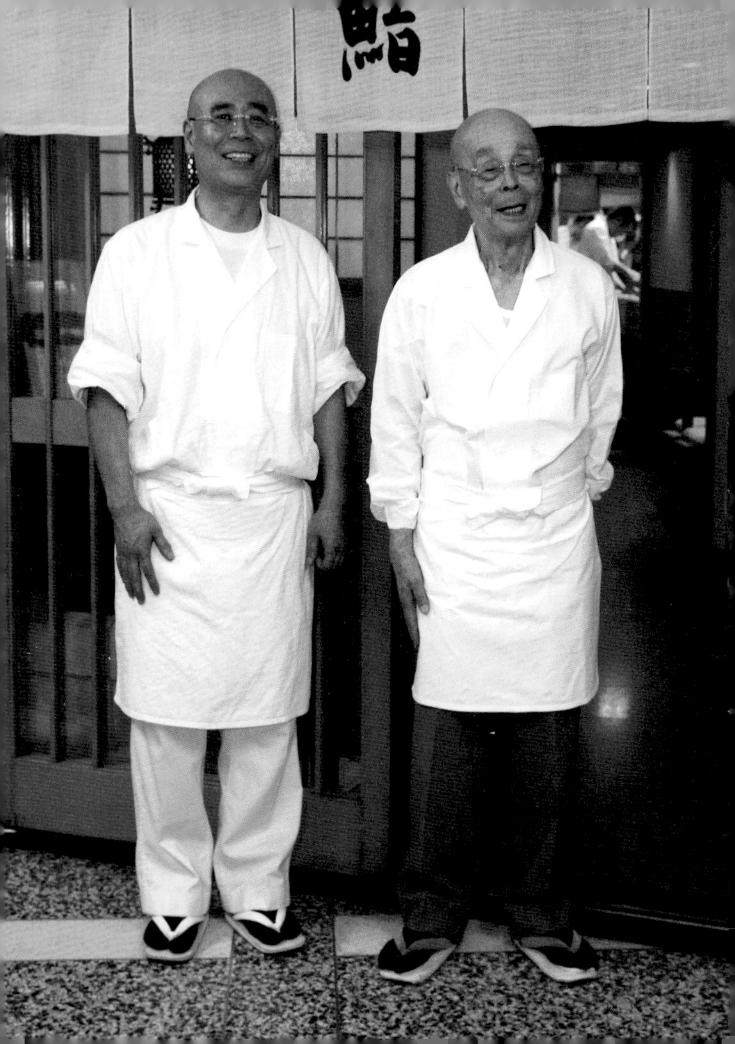

Visiting Sukiyabashi Jiro Again

Dining at Sukiyabashi Jiro is not like visiting a tourist
attraction. Different seasons bring different sushi, making
each visit unique. If you have enjoyed your experience
at Sukiyabashi Jiro, please be sure to come again.

SUKIYABASHI JIRO

Tsukamoto Sozan
Building Basement
4-2-15 Ginza
Chuo-ku, Tokyo, Japan
TEL 03-3535-3600
(+81-3-3535-3600 from abroad)

BUSINESS HOURS

11:30 a.m. to 2 p.m.
5:30 p.m. to 8 p.m.

すきやばし次郎
東京部中央区銀座 4-2-15
塚本素山ビル B1
電話：03-3535-3600

SUKIYABASHI JIRO ROPPONGI

6-12-2 Roppongi
Minato-ku, Tokyo, Japan
TEL 03-5413-6626
(+81-3-5413-6626 from abroad)

BUSINESS HOURS

11:30 a.m. to 2 p.m.
5:30 p.m. to 9 p.m.

すきやばし次郎　六本木
東京部港区六本木 6-12-2
電話：03-5413-6626

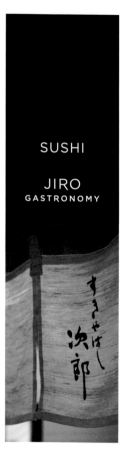

SUSHI: JIRO GASTRONOMY

BY Jiro Ono and Yoshikazu Ono
WITH SUPERVISION BY Masuhiro Yamamoto
WITH THANKS Sukiyabashi Jiro, Yosuke Suga, Haruna Eto
ORIGINAL DESIGN Atsushi Miyasaka
PHOTOGRAPHY Hiroshi Suga, Kenta Izumi

VIZ MEDIA EDITION

COVER & GRAPHIC DESIGN Shawn Carrico
EDITOR Leyla Aker

SUSHI SUKIYABASHI JIRO: JIRO GASTRONOMY
by Jiro ONO, Yoshikazu ONO
Supervision: Masuhiro YAMAMOTO
© 2014 Jiro ONO, Masuhiro YAMAMOTO
All rights reserved.
Original Japanese edition published by SHOGAKUKAN.
English translation rights in the United States of
America, Canada, the United Kingdom, Ireland,
Australia and New Zealand arranged with
SHOGAKUKAN.

Printed in Japan

Published by VIZ Media, LLC
P.O. Box 77010
San Francisco, CA 94107

10 9 8 7 6 5 4 3 2
First printing, October 2016
Second printing, February 2020

www.viz.com